The Nutcracker

From the story by E. T. A. Hoffmann
Illustrated by Doris Ettlinger

7373 North Cicero Avenue
Lincolnwood, Illinois 60712

Ground Floor, 59 Gloucester Place
London W1U 8JJ

Permission is never granted for commercial purposes.

Customer Service: 1-800-595-8484 or customer_service@pilbooks.com

www.pilbooks.com

p i kids is a trademark of Publications International, Ltd., and is registered in the United States.

8 7 6 5 4 3 2 1

Manufactured in China.

ISBN-13: 978-1-4508-5375-0

It was Christmas Eve. Fritz and Marie couldn't wait to open their presents. They hurried to the living room where the family Christmas tree was decorated with twinkling lights. On the floor were mountains of presents for the children. Marie and Fritz each picked up a wrapped gift.

"Wait, children," said their father. "We have to wait until Godfather Drosselmeier arrives."

Marie wondered how she could have forgotten about Godfather Drosselmeier. He always gave her and her brother the most wonderful gifts.

"What do you think Godfather Drosselmeier will bring us this year?" Marie asked.

The doorbell rang before anyone could answer. In walked Fritz and Marie's kindly godfather. He presented them both with a fantastic castle of golden towers and a collection of marching toy soldiers.

The children squealed with glee as they played with their new and enchanting gifts.

Then Marie spotted another gift off to the side. It looked like a little man.

"What is this?" Marie asked.

"Dear child," said Marie's father, "our friend here cracks nuts with his teeth." Marie placed a nut in the Nutcracker's mouth, and the little man bit it in two. Fritz chose the biggest nut, and with a CRACK, three teeth fell from the Nutcracker's mouth.

"Poor Nutcracker!" Marie cried. She bandaged his wounded mouth, and rocked him in her arms.

That night, Marie gently placed the Nutcracker in a glass cabinet. She was headed to bed when she heard squeaking, then marching.

"What could that be?" she wondered.

Marie looked and saw mice all over the room, forming ranks and preparing to attack the cabinet.

Suddenly, seven mouse heads with seven crowns rose up. This enormous mouse was the King of Mice. He led the mouse army toward the toy cabinet.

As the mice approached the cabinet, it began to glow. Then the doors opened up and out jumped the Nutcracker!

"Sound the advance!" the Nutcracker cried as he ran from the mice. With a clatter, Fritz's army of toy soldiers formed ranks on the floor, just like the army of mice.

Suddenly, guns were firing. The mice advanced. The battle raged on, and soon the Nutcracker was trapped!

The King of Mice charged right at the helpless Nutcracker.

Without thinking, Marie took off her slipper and threw it at the Mouse King.

Suddenly, Marie felt a sharp pain and fell to the floor.

When Marie awoke her mother was by her side.

"Oh, Mother," she said. "Have the mice gone away?"

"You fainted," said her mother.

Marie looked around the room.

She didn't see the mice or the toy soldiers.

"There was a battle between the dolls and the mice," Marie tried to tell her mom. But her mother thought it had all been a dream.

Godfather Drosselmeier came to visit later that day. He reached into his pocket and took out the Nutcracker, whose teeth and jaw he had mended. Then he placed the Nutcracker into the toy cabinet.

Later that night, Marie awoke to find the King of Mice on her nightstand, saying he would destroy the Nutcracker.

Marie went to the toy cabinet, found the Nutcracker, and told him what the Mouse King had said. The Nutcracker asked Marie for a sword. She slung Fritz's sword around his waist. Then she left the room as the two battled each other to the finish.

Marie could hear a lot of squeaking and fighting. Then the door opened, and there stood a handsome young man. The Nutcracker and his army had defeated the army of mice, and he had turned into a prince!

The prince explained that he was Godfather Drosselmeier's nephew.

He told Marie that a spell had turned him into a nutcracker. When he defeated the Mouse King and his army, the spell had been broken.

"Follow me," said the prince.

The prince led Marie to the hallway and through a secret passage that brought them to Candy Meadow.

Then the prince took Marie's hand and the two of them sailed down Honey River. The river led them to a tiny village.

"This is Gingerbread City," the prince told Marie. She admired the town of sweet treats and friendly people. The two of them continued down Honey River.

Finally, they arrived at Marzipan Castle, a beautiful palace with a hundred lofty towers. As the prince told Marie of his kingdom, she felt dizzy and then felt as though she were falling.

Again, Marie awoke in her own bed. Her mother was at her side, but the prince was nowhere to be seen. Marie tried to tell her mother about the Nutcracker and their marvelous journey. But her mother didn't believe her.

Then one day, Marie's mother told her that Godfather Drosselmeier was coming over, and he was bringing his nephew, too.

When Marie saw her godfather's nephew she knew he was the prince!

The prince asked Marie if she would come with him back to his kingdom.

"I would love to," she said, smiling.

The two lived happily ever after.